BUG BOOKS

Centipede

Karen Hartley, Chris Macro, and Philip Taylor

Heinemann Library
Chicago, Illinois

Customer Service 888-454-2279
Visit our website at www.heinemannraintree.com

Designed by Ron Kamen, Michelle Lisseter, and Bridge Creative Services Limited
Illustrations by Alan Fraser at Pennant Illustration
Printed in China by South China Printing Company

10 09 08 07 06
10 9 8 7 6 5 4 3 2 1

New edition ISBN: 1-4034-8295-0 (hardcover)
                   1-4034-8308-6 (paperback)

The Library of Congress has cataloged the first edition as follows:
Hartley, Karen, 1949-
        Centipede / Karen Hartley, Chris Macro, and Philip Taylor.
          p. cm. -- (Bug books)
        Includes bibliographical references and index.
        Summary: A simple introduction to the physical characteristics, diet, life cycle, predators,
                  habitat, and lifespan of centipedes.
        ISBN 1-57572-796-X (lib. bdg.)
        1. Centipedes—Juvenile literature. [1. Centipedes.] I. Macro, Chris, 1940-. II. Taylor,
        Philip, 1949-. III. Title. IV. Series.
      QL449.5.H28   1999
      595.6'2—dc21   98-42671
                            CIP
                            AC

Acknowledgments
The author and publishers are grateful to the following for permission to reproduce photographs:
Ardea: J Daniels pp. 17, 24, A Warren p. 19; Bruce Coleman Ltd: I Arndt p. 18, G Cubitt p. 8, C and D
Frith p. 10, A Purcell p. 14, Dr F Sauer p. 4; Corbis/DK Ltd: pp. 18, 20; Garden and Wildlife Matters:
pp. 5, 21, 23, 29; NHPA: R Fotheringham p. 22; Okapia: O Cabrero I Roura p. 15, U Gross p. 12;
Oxford Scientific Films: H Abipp p. 11, G Bernard pp. 7, 9, 27, 28, D Clyne/Mantis Wildlife Films p. 6,
J Cooke p. 25, Z Leszczynski/ Animals Animals p. 13, R Mendez/Animals Animals p. 16, P Parkes p. 26.

Cover photograph reproduced with permission of Photolibrary.com/Oxford Scientific Films/
John Mitchell.

The publishers would like to thank Nancy Harris for her assistance in the preparation of this book.

Every effort has been made to contact copyright holders of any material reproduced in this
book. Any omissions will be rectified in subsequent printings if notice is given to the publisher.

The paper used to print this book comes from sustainable sources.

Some words are shown in bold, **like this**. You can find out what they mean
by looking in the glossary.

Contents

What Are Centipedes?

Centipedes are small animals with lots of legs. They are invertebrates. This means they have no backbone.

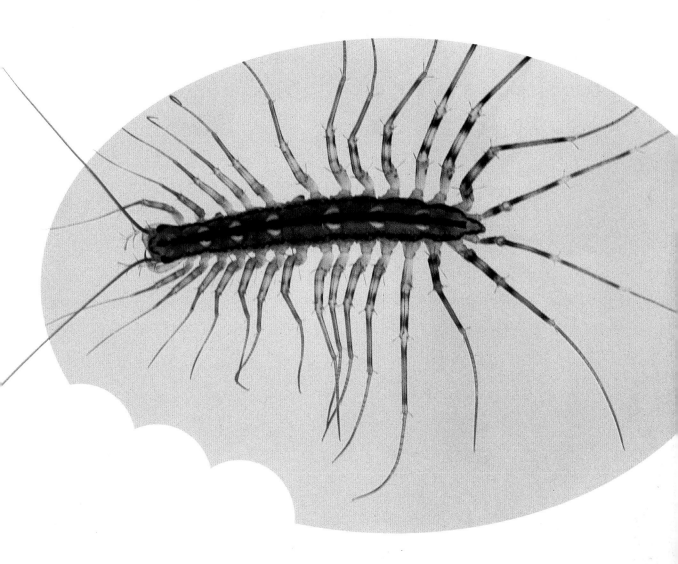

There are many different types
of centipedes. They live all over
the world.

5

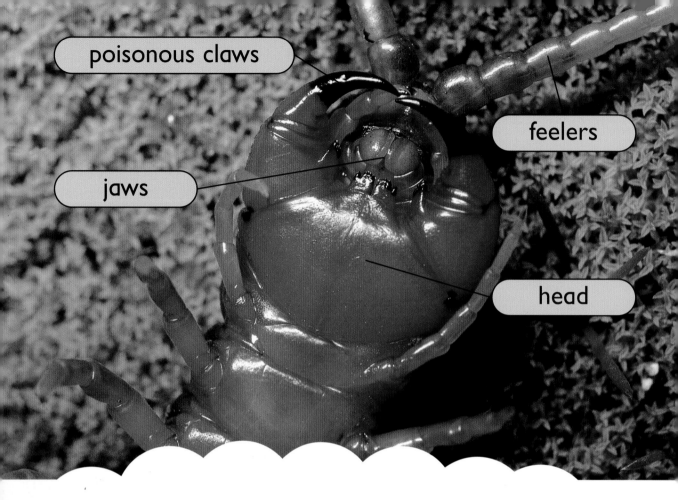

poisonous claws

feelers

jaws

head

Centipedes have long bodies. They have a head with a pair of **feelers**. They have big jaws for biting. There are two poisonous claws at the back of the head.

Centipedes' bodies are made up of
rings called **segments**. Each segment
has two legs. Centipedes are often dark
brown. If they live in the soil they are
pale brown.

Centipedes can be different sizes. The smallest centipedes have 15 pairs of legs. Big ones can have as many as 177 pairs.

Centipedes that live in cool countries can grow as long as your little finger. Centipedes that live in hot countries can be nearly as long as your arm.

How Are Centipedes Born?

In spring the **male** and **female** centipedes **mate**. The female lays eggs in a hole. She curls her body around her eggs to protect them.

eggs

A stone centipede rolls her eggs
in the soil. Little lumps of soil
stick to the eggs and hide them
from **predators**.

When the eggs **hatch** the centipedes are very small. The babies grow quickly and soon their skin is too small for them.

babies

They wriggle out of their old skins. There is a new skin underneath. This is called **molting**. The new skin has more body **segments** with new legs.

old skin

What Do Centipedes Eat?

Centipedes are **predators**. This means they hunt other small animals. They use their poisonous claws to kill worms, spiders and some insects.

This centipede is eating a moth.
Centipedes sometimes also eat
fruit or potatoes.

Which Animals Eat Centipedes?

Some creatures, such as large beetles, hunt centipedes. Some birds like to eat centipedes, too.

When we see blackbirds pecking the ground or digging with their beaks, they are looking for food. Sometimes they find a centipede to eat.

How Do Centipedes Move?

Centipedes have **joints** between their body **segments** so they can bend. Centipedes that live underground can wriggle into tiny cracks.

Some centipedes can move very quickly. They use their longer back legs to push themselves forward.

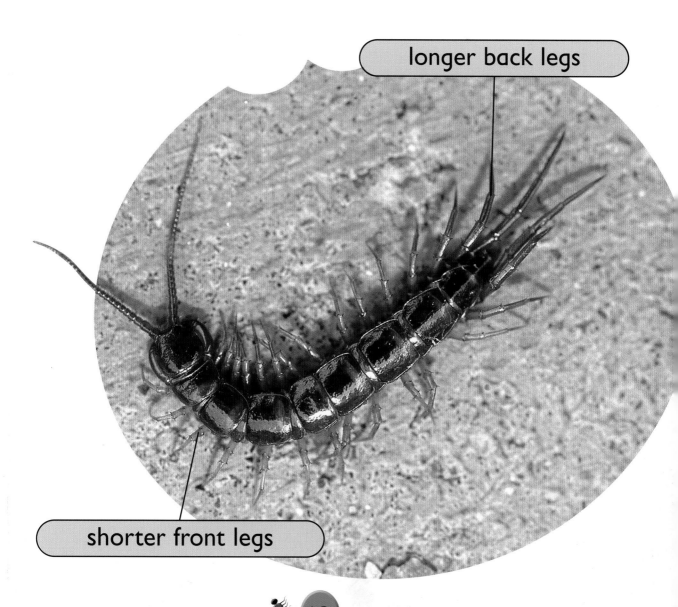

longer back legs

shorter front legs

Where Do Centipedes Live?

Centipedes like to live where it is damp and out of the sun. Some of the big centipedes live in hot rainforests.

In gardens, centipedes live under
stones or under a shed. They can live
in a pile of leaves or a rotting log.
Others live in the soil.

How Long Do Centipedes Live?

If they are safe and warm,
centipedes can live for more
than five years.

Sometimes centipedes cannot find enough food to eat in the winter. They sleep underground until warmer weather comes. This is called **hibernating**.

What Do Centipedes Do?

Most centipedes are helpful to gardeners. They kill many garden **pests**. Pests harm garden plants.

Some centipedes give a painful, poisonous bite if they are angry or upset.

How Are Centipedes Special?

Centipedes are **nocturnal**. This means they usually only come out at night. This is because the sun dries out their skin.

Some centipedes have no eyes. When the creatures they hunt move, they make a shaking movement called **vibrations**. Centipedes smell and taste with their **feelers**.

feelers

Thinking About Centipedes

Remember that some centipedes cannot see. How do you think they find their way around?

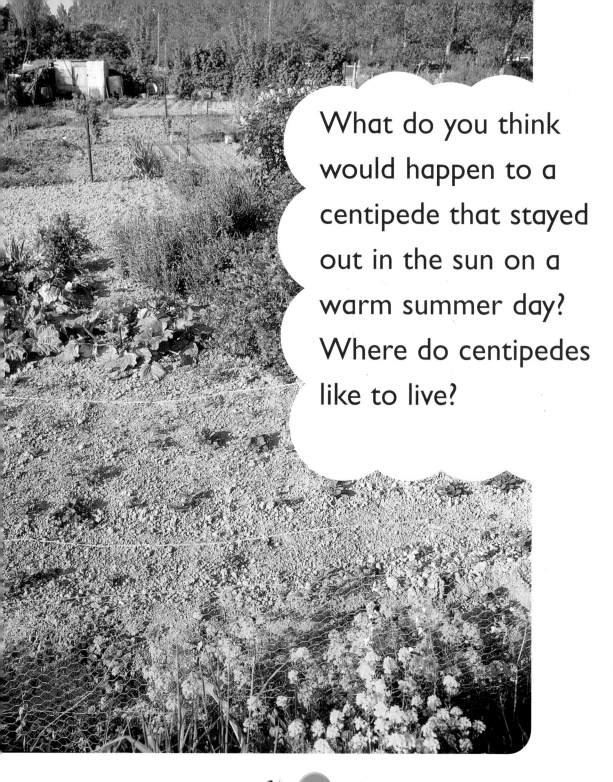

What do you think would happen to a centipede that stayed out in the sun on a warm summer day? Where do centipedes like to live?

Bug Map

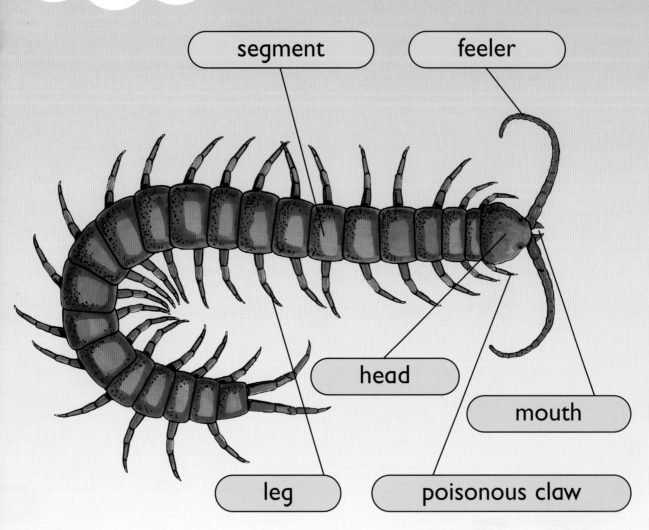

segment

feeler

head

mouth

poisonous claw

leg

Actual size

Glossary

feelers thin growths from the head of a centipede that help it to feel, smell and taste

female girl

hatch to come out of an egg

hibernating sleeping through the winter months

joint part of the body that lets it bend

male boy

mate when male and female centipedes make baby centipedes

molt when a centipede grows too big for its skin it grows a new one and wriggles out of its old skin

nocturnal an animal that sleeps in the day and comes out at night

pests animals that are a nuisance to people

predator animal that hunts other animals

segments small pieces of the body that are joined together one after the other

vibration shaking that happens in the air or on the ground when an animal moves

Index

More Books to Read

Dickmann, Nancy. *Centipedes*. Chicago: Raintree, 2006.